APPLYING

THE BLOOD

OF JESUS

100 Powerful Declarations to Activate the
Mystery and Miracles of the Blood of
Jesus

DANIEL C. OKPARA

TO EDIFY, HEAL, AND BLESS

The author provides the content of this book in good faith: to enlighten, encourage, and heal. He believes that when the subject discussed is followed, it will produce healing, divine intervention, and miracles from God. However, he does not intend his revelations to replace professional counseling and suggestions in your life. Neither is the teaching in this book supposed to be a doctrine to alter your faith in Christ. The author is sure and believes you will be blessed reading this book. However, he will bear no responsibility for any adverse consequences from any wrong understanding and application of the subject taught in this material. He prays that you will use the teaching well and increase your faith in God.

Published By:

Better Life Media.

BETTER LIFE WORLD OUTREACH CENTER.

Website: www.BetterLifeWorld.org

Email: info@betterlifeworld.org

FOLLOW ON FACEBOOK

www.facebook.com/drdanielokpara

This title and others are available for quantity discounts, gifts, and evangelism. Email us for inquiries.

All texts, calls, letters, testimonies, and inquiries are welcome.

BE EMPOWERED ON SOCIAL MEDIA

Today, God says...

"He has begun a good work in your life, and He will bring it to perfection. He will not abandon you half way. Yes, you have had problems, drawbacks, challenges, and red sea situations, but He will see you through. Your setback is temporary. It is a setup for God's work in your life. Only believe. Everything about you will end in praise."

DR. DANIEL OKPARA | WORD4TODAY | DAY 235

Are you looking for resources to keep your spirit on fire? Follow me on Facebook for powerful streams and prayers to stir your heart for Jesus and command your breakthrough every day.

www.facebook.com/drdanielokpara

RECEIVE WEEKLY PRAYERS

Powerful Prayers Sent to Your Inbox Every Monday

Enter your email address to receive notifications of new posts, prayers and prophetic declarations sent to you by email.

Email Address

Sign Me Up

Go to Breakthrough Prayers to subscribe for my free weekly prayer points and prophetic declarations sent to you by email.

www.betterlifeworld.org/breakthrough-prayers

FREE BOOKS

Download these POWERFUL books from my website and take your relationship with God to a new level.

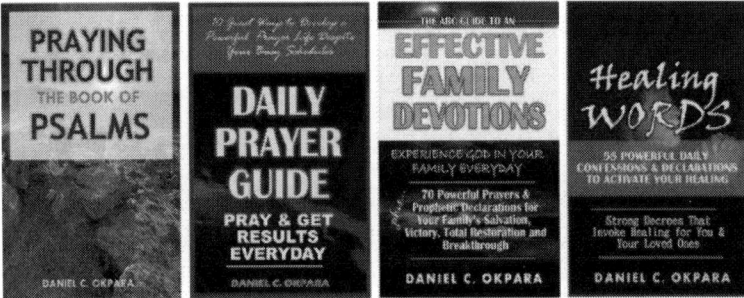

The link to download the books are at the end of this book.

CONTENTS

Chapter 7: All-Around Blessings By the Blood of Jesus

Introduction

Luke 22:19-20 (PT) - .Then he lifted a loaf, and after praying a prayer of thanksgiving to God, he gave each of his apostles a piece of bread, saying, "This loaf is my body, which is now offered to you. Always eat it to remember me."

. After supper, he lifted the cup again and said, "This cup is my blood of the new covenant I make with you, and it will be poured out soon for all of you.

This is my third book on the blood of Jesus Christ. In my first two books, *How God Taught Me to Pray the Blood of Jesus* and *The Mystery of the Holy Communion*, I shared some personal encounters that challenged me to see the blood of Jesus Christ as an instrument of spiritual warfare.

"When the blood is activated, the enemy takes to his heels."

In this book, I want to challenge you to activate the power of the blood of Jesus in your life through the mystery of the Holy Communion and declaration prayers. Take the Holy Communion nonstop for seven days and make these powerful blood of Jesus declarations. Something mysterious will happen in your life. You will witness miracles and experience supernatural encounters and transformations.

Our knowledge of the blood of Jesus must go beyond Sunday school class topics. We must experience its power to save, heal, deliver, and open doors. This is what this book will provoke in your life.

From the opening verses above, the Holy Communion is a medium for worshipping God, walking in obedience, and invoking the blessings of God, such as healing, deliverance, and protection. It is not just an activity designed to be part of our religious practice once in a while. It is to be taken often – regularly. The more you take in it with understanding, the more of its blessings will manifest in your life.

So, I welcome you to this seven days Holy Communion Challenge, a Holy Ghost-inspired prayer challenge designed to meditate on the blood of Jesus, take the Holy Communion, and declare the blood of Jesus Christ over our lives for seven days and nights.

- The blood of Jesus is the price of our salvation and redemption from sin and death.

- The blood of Jesus is the source of our protection.

- The blood of Jesus is our shield. When we declare the blood, a spiritual wall is erected to shield us from enemy attacks.

- The blood of Jesus is the means for our healing. By His stripes, we are healed – physically, emotionally, and spiritually.

- The blood of Jesus is the basis of our victory. When we apply the blood to our situations, we take authority over the devil and his works.

- The blood of Jesus is the negotiator of our cleansing. When we confess our sins and apply the blood of Jesus to our hearts and minds, we are washed clean and made pure in God's sight.

- The blood of Jesus is the channel of God's blessings. When we receive communion and declare the blood of Jesus over our lives, we open the door to God's abundant grace and favor.

In this book, we will take the Communion for seven days and nights and make 100 plus scriptural declarations based on the blood of Jesus Christ. These declarations are not just some positive words to motivate you; they are potent codes that will activate the power of the blood of Jesus in your life.

How to Use the Book

I recommend these prayer-declarations every morning and night. Before you make them, prepare tokens to symbolize the flesh and blood of Jesus Christ. They can be bread (for

His flesh) and wine (for His blood). Then choose a chapter, and declare with faith and passion.

As you take the communion in the morning, declare some of the prayers with it. Then do the same at night – especially at midnight.

Each chapter has a theme related to a specific area of God's promise. Each topic has several scriptures personalized for declaration and associated with the blood of Jesus. These declarations of blessings grounded in the blood of Jesus will ignite faith, confidence, and expectation in your heart. They will activate the power in the blood of Jesus Christ in your life.

Voice these declarations with passion and authority, knowing that the power of the blood of Jesus has already secured these blessings for you. And while praying and declaring the scriptures in this book, also follow the words the Holy Spirit will drop in your heart. Pray with intensity.

As you make the declarations with faith and expectation, you will encounter God in the most unusual way because the blood of Jesus is God's greatest gift to man. You will see things happening. You will see breakthroughs and many miracles manifesting.

Let's start by declaring together: "The blood of Jesus Christ has redeemed me from the power of sin and death."

MEDITATE ON THIS

"The blood of Jesus is the basis of our victory. When we apply the blood to our situations, we take authority over the devil and his works."

Chapter 1

Redeemed By the Blood of Jesus

Ephesians 1:7 – *"In him, I have redemption through his blood, the forgiveness of my sins, in accordance with the riches of God's grace."*

The blood of Jesus is the foundation of my redemption. Through His sacrifice, I have been redeemed from the power of sin and death. I stand reconciled to God.

Today, as I meditate on the power of Christ's blood and declare its blessing in my life, I will walk in the fullness of His redemption and love.

I declare that I am bought at a price; I will honor God with my life because the blood of Jesus has redeemed me.

As I take the Holy Communion today, I declare the power of the blood of Jesus in my life. His sacrifice has set me free from the power of sin and death.

Declarations

The Word of God is true, eternal, powerful, and sharper than any double-edged sword. The Word permeates into the spirit, soul, and body and brings about the life of God in man. As I declare these scriptures, I am eating the flesh of Jesus and drinking His blood. His life will become real in me and through me.

1. **Colossians 1:13-14** – "God has delivered me from the power of darkness and ushered me into the kingdom of His Son, in whom I have redemption and the

forgiveness of sins. By the blood of Jesus, I now live and move in the fullness of Christ's salvation and grace.

2. **Romans 3:24** – "Jesus paid the price for my sins and reconciled me with God. I am no longer burdened by the guilt and shame of my past. The blood of Jesus has broken the chains that once bound me; the blood has delivered me to live a life free from the grip of sin. I now enjoy a transformative liberty that enables me to walk in the fullness of God's grace.

The grace of God freely justifies me. My justification is not achieved through any work or personal efforts; it is a gift bestowed upon me through the blood of Jesus.

Today and for all the days to come, I walk in the assurance that I am justified, accepted, and deeply loved by my Heavenly Father, in Jesus' name.

3. **Galatians 3:13** – "Christ has delivered me from the curse of the law by taking it upon Himself. I am free from the punishment of any inputted or inherited sins. I now live in the abundance of God's grace, mercy, and freedom."

4. **1 Peter 1:18-19** – "Christ has redeemed me from my past empty way of life through His precious blood. He is the Lamb without blemish who gave His life for me. I now walk in the fullness of His holiness."

5. **Hebrews 9:12** – "Through His blood, Jesus obtained eternal redemption for us. He entered the Most Holy Place once and for all so I can approach God with confidence. I bear no more guilt and shame in me. By this communion today, I

confidently approach the throne of God and declare grace and help for me, in Jesus' name."

6. **1 Corinthians 6:20** – "Christ bought me at the price of His precious blood. My salvation is a very costly gift to me. I will never forget this. I willingly commit myself to honor God with my body, soul, and spirit."

7. **Revelation 5:9** – "I declare that my life has been redeemed by the precious blood of Jesus Christ. The life I live now is no longer mine. It is Christ's. I am a part of the redeemed saints. All my praise and flory belongs to Jesus Christ, my Lord, and Savior, who was slain for me. I will walk in the fullness of the knowledge of His redemption and my victory daily, in Jesus' name."

8. **Isaiah 44:22** – "I declare that God has swept away my offenses and my sins through the blood of Jesus. I am redeemed by the Lord, and I declare my praise and thanksgiving to Him. My worship belongs to Him forever and ever.

9. **Psalm 130:7-8** – "With the Lord Jesus is unconditional love and absolute freedom. He has redeemed me and set me free by His blood. From this day forward, I will walk in the assurance of my salvation in Him."

10. **Titus 2:14** – "Jesus, You gave Yourself for me, to redeem me from all wickedness and to purify me for Yourself. Please help me be eager to follow You from this day onwards, doing what is good and fulfilling Your purpose for my life."

11. **1 John 1:7** – "I declare that as I walk in the light of Jesus, His blood purifies my conscience and grants me fellowship with Him and His people. Every day, I am cleansed by His blood."

12. **Hebrews 10:19-22** – "I declare that I have the confidence to enter the Most Holy place by the blood of Jesus. He opened a new and living way for me through His death and resurrection. He is the great High Priest over the house of God. Today and every day, I draw near to God with a sincere heart and full assurance of faith, knowing that the blood of Jesus cleanses me from a guilty conscience and washes me with pure water. I will live and walk in His presence every day filled with hope, love, peace, and favor."

13. **Revelation 1:5-6** – "I declare that God loves me. Through the blood of Jesus

Christ, my sinful nature and past sins are washed away. I am now a part of Christ's kingdom, called to fulfill His purpose on earth. He has made me a priest to serve and be a faithful witness of His Word. My praise is unto Him forever and ever."

14. **Ephesians 2:13** – "Through the blood of Christ, I am brought near to God. I was once far away from Him, but now I am His child and a part of His family. I walk in the full assurance of His closeness to me."

15. **Hebrews 13:20-21** – "God has brought me back from the dead through the blood of Christ's eternal covenant. He has equipped me with everything good to do His will, and He is working in me to do what pleases Him daily. To Him be glory forever and ever."

16. **1 Corinthians 11:26** – "Every time I eat His flesh and drink His blood, I declare the Lord's death until He comes. As I partake of the bread and the cup, I remember His sacrifice and receive the totality of His life in me, even as I eagerly await His glorious return."

17. **Revelation 1:5** – "Again, I declare that Jesus loves me and has freed me from my past by His blood. I am now a child of God, redeemed and cherished by God."

18. **1 John 1:7** – "From today, I will walk in the light of Christ. His blood continually cleanses me. I am purified and made whole. I now live a life of victory over the works of darkness."

19. **Colossians 1:20** – "Through Christ, all things on earth and heaven are reconciled to God. Yes, Christ made peace through

His blood shed on the cross. I am now a part of that reconciliation, and I walk in the assurance of my peace with God.

20. **Romans 5:9** – "I am justified by Christ's blood; I am saved from God's wrath through Him. I am made righteous by His atonement; I am fully under His care and protection."

Thank You, Jesus!

MEDITATE ON THIS

"Through the blood of Christ, you are brought near to God. You are no longer far away from Him. You are now His child and a part of His family. Therefore, walk in the full assurance of His closeness to you."

Chapter 2

All-Round Protection By the Blood of Jesus

Revelation 12:11 – *"By the blood of the Lamb, Jesus Christ, and the word of my testimony, I have conquered the devil and his agents. I do not love my life more than following Jesus."*

As a believer in Christ, I know this world is in gross darkness, full of attacks and dangers. However, the blood of Jesus is the greatest weapon against the forces of darkness. The blood is my shield and protection. As I declare the blood today and represent it with the Holy Communion, I have victory and protection from the enemy, his agents, and their activities. I am safe from every harm, danger, and enemy attack.

Declarations

The Word of God is true, eternal, powerful, and sharper than any double-edged sword. The Word permeates into the spirit, soul, and body and brings about the life of God in man. As I declare these scriptures today, I am eating the flesh of Jesus and drinking His blood. His life will become real in me and through me.

1. **Psalm 91:1-2** – "I declare that I live in the safe and secret place of the Most High. I rest under the comforting shadow of the Almighty. The Lord is my refuge, my fortress, and my protector. He protects me from every attack; my dwelling place is secure and in peace, in Jesus' name.

2. **Psalm 121:7-8** – "By the blood of Jesus Christ, the Lord will keep me from every harm. He will watch over my life, observing my every step, now and forever, and causing me to rest in the abundance of His provision."

3. **Isaiah 54:17** – "Any weapon formed to harm me will fail, and any tongue raised against me, in judgment, shall be condemned. This is my heritage in Christ. My vindication comes from the Almighty Himself. By the blood of Jesus, I am walking in divine protection and victory."

4. **Psalm 18:2** – "O Lord, You are my solid rock, my invisible fortress, and my redeemer in times of distress. You are the solid foundation upon which I stand, my trustworthy shield, my salvation, and the stronghold of my life."

5. **Psalm 138:7** – "By the blood of Jesus Christ, I declare that I and my household will be preserved through troubled times because God is holding our very existence. By His outstretched arm, He will quench the fury of our adversaries, and with His mighty right hand, He will deliver us from every evil. By the communion of Christ's flesh and blood, we will enjoy divine protection every day, in Jesus' name.

6. **Psalm 121:3-4** – "By the blood of Jesus, my heavenly Father is guiding and shielding me. I will never stumble or fall, for He is my keeper. As He faithfully watches over Israel, He also watches over me with the same unwavering vigilance. I will confidently go about my daily business because I am secure in His constant protection.

7. **Proverbs 18:10** – "Lord Jesus, Your name is a strong tower, and I, made righteous by Your blood, declare my security in Your name. I trust in Your consummate power to preserve me from every danger and spiritual ambush, in Jesus' name.

8. **2 Thessalonians 3:3** – "By the precious blood of Jesus Christ, I declare that the Lord is faithful to strengthen and protect me from all the schemes and attacks of the evil one. I trust in His unfailing love and power to keep me safe and protected, and I declare that no enemy can overcome me because I am hidden in Christ."

9. **Psalm 34:7** – "As I worship and serve the Lord, His angel surrounds and shields me everyday. He will always rescue me from any trouble, in Jesus' name.

10. **Psalm 125:2** – "I declare that as the mountains surround Jerusalem, so the Lord surrounds me and my family, both now and always."

11. **Psalm 27:1** – "Because the Lord is my light and my salvation, I will fear no one. He is the stronghold of my life, so I shall not live in fear. I stand on His word and forbid the spirit of fear from my heart, soul, and body, in Jesus' name."

12. **Psalm 46:1-3** – "God is my strength and my refuge; He is a constant help in times of need. Therefore, I won't accept anxiety and fear in my heart. Even if the earth disappears and the mountains fall into the depths of the sea, I am always protected by the blood of Jesus."

13. **Isaiah 41:10** – God is saying to me today, [Insert your name] "I am your God;

don't be afraid or discouraged. I will support and help you; I will keep you with my righteous right hand."

14. **Psalm 34:19** – "By the precious blood of Jesus Christ, I have been made righteous before God. Even when the righteous has many troubles, God delivers him from them all. I, therefore, decree and declare complete deliverance in every aspect of my life.

15. **Psalm 91:4** – "God is covering me with his feathers, and under his wings, I have a lifetime refuge; his faithfulness is my shield and bulletproof. I will dwell in His presence and walk in His grace and loving-kindness."

16. **Proverbs 3:25-26** – "Because of the blood of Jesus Christ, I have no fear, and I will never have any fear of unexpected

disasters, or of the destruction that reaches the wicked, for the Lord is always on my side and will always deliver and keep my foot from every snare."

17.   **Isaiah 54:14** – "The righteousness of God credited to me through the blood of Jesus Christ establishes my foundation and protection against every demonic tyranny and oppression. I, therefore, declare today that evil is banished from my dwelling. There is no more room for anxiety, fear, and distress in my life and family, in Jesus' name."

18.   **Nahum 1:7** – "I declare that the Lord is good; He is my sanctuary all the days of my life, both in good times and bad times. He cares for me because I trust in him."

19.   **Psalm 37:28** – "God loves me and every member of my household. He will

never forsake us. May those who attempt evil against us be wholly destroyed. By the blood of Jesus Christ, may the evil they try against us befall them and their descendants, in Jesus' name."

20. **Psalm 5:11** – "I declare that I take solace in the Lord. I will rejoice and be glad in Him. I will sing for joy every day because He spreads His protection as a net over me and my family.

I am grateful for the mystery of protection at work in my life through the blood of Jesus. With each declaration I made today, I accept the total security of Christ's blood. May this truth be firmly rooted in my heart, enabling me to live fearlessly and victoriously every day, in Jesus' name.

Amen.

MEDITATE ON THIS

"God has made you righteous through the precious blood of Jesus Christ. He will deliver you, his righteous, from every trouble you face. Today, you have complete and total protection and deliverance."

Chapter 3

Healed By the Blood of Jesus

Isaiah 53:5 – *"By the stripes of Jesus, I am healed. He bore all my sicknesses and diseases on the cross. His blood flows through my veins, bringing me new life and complete wholeness. Every affliction and infirmity must leave my life today and forever. By the blood of Jesus, I am healed, restored, and made whole."*

J esus was pierced and crushed for my sins. The punishment He faced on the Cross is for my peace, health, and abundant life.

Today, as I take the Holy Communion, I imagine myself at the foot of the cross. I see my Lord, Jesus Christ, as He is crucified. Blood drips from His hands, feet, and side. He looks at me and proclaims, *"My child, it is finished!"* and gives up His spirit.

What Jesus did at the Cross, He did for me. When He said, *"It is finished,"* He spoke of my salvation and deliverance from the power of Satan. He took my sins, sicknesses, and sorrows on Himself. He made the sacrifice for my complete redemption.

I now eat His flesh and drink His blood today with the perfect understanding that His blood is for my healing. This Communion – the flesh and blood – that I eat and drink washes away my infirmities and afflictions and heals my body, mind, heart, and soul. The flesh and blood go to the deepest parts of my wounds and makes me whole. And by the blood of

Jesus Christ, I receive power to walk in divine health, in Jesus' name.

Declarations

As I declare these scriptures and embrace them, I will be empowered, healed, and transformed by the power of the Word. By the blood of Jesus Christ, I will walk in the fullness of healing, restoration, and divine health.

1. **Psalm 103:2-3** – "O my soul, give thanks to the Lord and never forget all the blessings He has bestowed upon me. He is the one who pardons all my transgressions and heals all my afflictions."

2. **Isaiah 40:29-31** – "I declare that God Himself is my strength. When I am weak, He makes me strong. When I am exhausted and shattered, He revives me with His power. When I stumble and fall, He renews me, for

my trust is in Him. I will soar above my troubles like an eagle and run my race without growing weary or fainting. By His grace, I will keep moving forward, confident that He will sustain me.

3. **Psalm 147:3** – "God heals my broken heart and binds up all my secret and open wounds. I am restored to perfect health - mentally, spiritually, emotionally, and physically, in Jesus' name."

4. **Jeremiah 30:17** – "You, O Lord, my God, will restore me to complete health and heal all my wounds, for You have declared it. Even when I may feel like an outcast, forgotten by the world around me, You, God, see and care deeply for me. You will not leave me in my brokenness. You will wrap me in Your loving arms and make me whole again.

In the Mighty name of Jesus Christ, I declare that every wound in my body, mind, and spirit is healed by the power of the blood of Jesus. Henceforth, I will arise as a testimony to the goodness and grace of God."

5. **James 5:14-15** – "Thank You, Lord, for the many provisions You have made for the healing of Your people. Thank You for the opportunity to pray a prayer of agreement with the elders of the church. Thank you for the communion and its power to work through my physical and spiritual health. As I use this communion to connect with You today, I ask for total healing and restoration. If there are physical steps I need to take to activate my healing, may Your Spirit guide me to those You have sent to make such instructions clear to me. May we connect and enforce Your healing and health plan for me and my family, in Jesus' name."

6. **Psalm 107:20** – "Jesus is the Word of God sent for my healing and deliverance from destruction. As I eat His flesh and drink His blood, His word is planted in me forever. Therefore, I declare that I am healed and delivered from the grave. I am healed and delivered from every demonic oppression. From now onwards, I will walk in the fullness of Christ's resurrection power and healing, secured by His blood, in Jesus' name."

7. **Matthew 8:17** – "Jesus, You willingly took upon Yourself my infirmities and bore my diseases. You carried them upon Your own body on the cross so that I might be free from the bondage of sickness and disease. By Your wounds, I am healed. This is an eternal truth. I will walk in its reality. My life is redeemed from sickness and destruction by the blood of Jesus Christ."

8. **1 Peter 2:24** – "Thank You, Jesus. You carried my sins in Your body on the cross. You forgave me even before I was born. I am righteous through Your grace. By Your wounds, I am healed.

"Today, I declare that I no longer live in bondage to sin or sickness; I walk in the freedom and wholeness that Your blood has purchased for me."

9. **Exodus 15:26** – "Precious Holy Spirit, please help me attentively listen to Your voice and obey Your commands. Through my submission, partnership, and declared obedience to You, shield me from diseases and infirmities. May divine health flow through me daily as I align myself with Your will, in Jesus' name."

10. **Psalm 91:9-10** – "I declare before heaven and earth, before men and spirits, before the

seen and unseen worlds: the Lord is my refuge and dwelling place. He is my safety and protection. The blood of Jesus Christ is a wall over my life and family. Therefore, no harm or disaster will overtake or overwhelm me. I am shielded from all evil, in Jesus' name."

11. **Mark 11:23** — "Standing on the divine privilege provided through the Holy Communion, and the authority of the Scriptures, I speak to every mountain of sickness, disease, and affliction in my life. I speak to every pain, sorrow, anxiety, fear, and attack. I command them to be uprooted, cast into the sea, and never return.

"I declare that by my spoken words of faith and declaration, I receive the manifestation of healing and restoration in every area of my life, in Jesus' name."

12. **Romans 8:11** – "The same Holy Spirit who raised Jesus from the dead resides within me. His resurrection power quickens my mortal body and brings life to every cell, tissue, and organ. By the blood of Jesus Christ, I walk in the energy and strength that come from the Holy Spirit's indwelling, in Jesus' name."

13. **2 Corinthians 1:20** – "According to the scriptures, every promise of God finds its fulfillment in Christ. All the promises of healing, restoration, and divine health in Him are 'Yes' and 'Amen.' I speak forth the 'Amen' to these promises, declaring them with faith and certainty. The Holy Communion I take today binds the manifestation of this "Amen" in my life, in Jesus' name."

14. **Psalm 30:5** – "I declare that I will not remain in a place of mourning. Joy comes to me with the morning light. In His faithfulness,

God has turned my tears into dancing. He has taken off my sackcloth and clothed me with gladness. May His name be praised forever."

15. **Psalm 139:14** – "I am fearfully and wonderfully made. O God, You formed me in my mother's womb and know every detail of my life. I am not a mistake. I am not ordinary. I am not a failure. I am valuable to heaven and to the earth. I am valuable to You, my creator, and I am grateful for Your works in my life.

16. **Romans 8:32** – "Father, You did not withhold Yourself, Your own Son, but graciously gave Yourself up for my sake; how much more will You not also provide for my every need? Your provision extends to my healing, restoration, and divine health. Today, with Communion as a remembrance of Your death on the Cross, I receive with gratitude every good thing that You graciously bestow

upon me through the blood of Jesus, in Jesus' name.

17. **Psalm 119:93** – "I declare my commitment to never forget the Words of God, His precepts, and promises. For through His Words, He preserves and sustains my life. As I declare the word, I receive help from the Holy Spirit to meditate on it and walk in complete obedience. Thank You, Father.

18. **Proverbs 3:7-8** – "In the name of Jesus Christ, I embrace the connection between my spiritual posture and physical well-being. I humbly submit myself to the wisdom and guidance of the Lord, God, Almighty. I acknowledge that my understanding is limited. I cannot fashion my own ways and manage my life by myself. I need God every day.

Therefore, Holy Spirit, plant the reverential fear of God in my heart day to day. As I walk in Your fear, may Your divine wisdom impart health to my body and nourishment to my bones. By the blood of Jesus Christ, my daily strength and vitality are established, in Jesus' name.

19. **Mark 11:24** – "I declare, according to the Word of God, I have received everything I asked and decreed in this prayer meeting. Through the blood of Jesus, I walk in the assurance of this knowledge: I am healed and healthy, and I live a prosperous life in Christ.

20. **Psalm 30:2** – "Thank You, Lord, for my healing. I called upon you, and you healed me. I declare my gratitude to You. Receive all the glory, today and always, in Jesus' name."

MEDITATE ON THIS

"God heals your broken heart and binds up all your secret and open wounds. You are restored to perfect health - mentally, spiritually, emotionally, and physically, in Jesus' name."

Chapter 4

Victory By the Blood of Jesus

Revelation 12:11 – *"I have overcome the devil and his agents through the blood of the Lamb and the power of my testimony. My love for Christ surpasses my passion for life, and I follow Him wholeheartedly, no matter the cost. With faith and trust in God, I declare that I am victorious over all the schemes of the adversary, and I will continue to stand secure.*

The blood of Jesus redeems, protects, cleanses, and gives us victory over the enemy. So, I announce today that I overcome the devil and his schemes by the blood of the Lamb and the declarations of my mouth. As I meditate on the victory that the blood of Jesus has won for me, take the Holy Communion, and declare the Word, God's power is activated for my victory over any issue and obstacle in my life, in Jesus' name.

Declarations

The Word of God is true, eternal, powerful, and sharper than any double-edged sword. The Word permeates into the spirit, soul, and body and brings about the life of God in man. As I declare these scriptures today, I am eating the flesh of Jesus and drinking His blood. His life will become real in me and through me.

1. **1 Corinthians 15:57** – "I thank You, Father, for activating my victory through Christ. By His blood, You made me holy and victorious over sin and death. Today, I declare the reality of my victory and proclaim that I

am an overcomer. I have overcome every obstacle and challenge in my life. I live a triumphant life, in the name of Jesus Christ."

2. Colossians 2:14-15 —"Christ has canceled all satanic charges against me by His blood. He has nullified all the legal indebtedness against me and my destiny. He has disarmed the powers and authorities that stood against us. He made this victory and divine cancelation public, disarmed these evil powers, and triumphed over them by His death at the Cross.

"Today, as I take the Holy Communion, I remind myself that God has given me victory over the devil. I am not fighting because Christ has already won the battle. I am only declaring what He has done for me. I am victorious over the works of the devil today and all the days of my life."

3. Revelation 1:5b-6 – "Jesus loves me. He has freed me from my sins by shedding His blood on the cross, and made me a member of His kingdom. He has given me the privilege to serve God as His child. I am now a priest called after the order of the apostles, prophets, and kings. I am a seed of the King, and I reign with Christ.

4. 1 John 4:4 – "I am a child of God. He who is in me is far greater than everything in the world. I am empowered by the Holy Spirit. He has anointed and imbued me with His strength, strategy, and guidance to overcome any obstacle. By the blood of Jesus, I stand firm in my faith and claim victory over any storms in my life right now."

4. 1 Peter 1:18-19 – "The blood of Jesus has redeemed me from the empty way of life I once lived. I now live in the richness of God's grace. I was not redeemed with perishable things like silver or gold but with the precious blood of Jesus, a Lamb without blemish or defect. I will always walk in this knowledge and the victory of my redemption by the blood.

5. Hebrews 10:19 – "By the blood of Jesus, I have the confidence to enter the Most Holy Place and approach God with boldness. Spiritual bondage, legalism, and tradition are broken. Christ leads me daily in a triumphal procession toward heavenly encounters and blessings. I spread the aroma of the knowledge of Him everywhere I go, in Jesus' name."

6. 1 Corinthians 6:20 – "By the Communion that I take this day, I declare that the blood of Jesus has bought me with a price. I belong to God and God alone. No demonic power has right over me. I am in Christ, and Christ is in me. All other connections, covenants, agreements, and commitments are permanently destroyed, in the mighty name of Jesus Christ."

7. Zechariah 9:11 – "The blood of Jesus established a new covenant with me. Through it, I am freed from the sin and consequence of disobedience of the first covenant. The blood has released me from the waterless pit and has given me an eternal inheritance. I walk in the power of the new covenant and the victory of the blood of Jesus Christ."

8. 1 John 5:4 – "I am born of God. I have victory over the world. My faith in Christ empowers me to live a life of victory over the works of darkness. I triumph in every area of my life, in Jesus' name."

9. 1 Peter 2:10 – "By faith, I declare that I have been purchased for God by the precious blood of Jesus Christ. I belong to the redeemed of the Lord from every tribe, language, people, and nation. Though once I was not a people, now I am the people of God. I live in the fullness of Christ's victory daily, having received His mercy and grace. By the Holy Spirit, I am empowered to live a meaningful and purposeful life, knowing that God has chosen and set me apart. Nothing can separate me from His love. He will lead me daily to triumph in every situation."

10. Revelation 19:13-16 – "Lord Jesus, I declare my faith in you as my King and Lord. I believe You are the Word of God, riding on a white horse with eyes like blazing fire, wearing a robe dipped in blood, to save me from sin and the power of Satan. Thank You for Your sacrifice and for writing Your name in my heart.

"By today's Communion, Lord Jesus, I remind myself that You died for me and that You will come again to reign as King. I am part of the armies of heaven, washed by Your blood, dressed in fine linen, white and clean, following you on a white horse. I submit my life to Your authority and trust in You completely. Help me to follow you faithfully and serve you wholeheartedly. May your kingdom come; may your will be done on earth, in my life, and in my family, as it is done in heaven, in your holy name, I pray.

11. Revelation 7:14 – "The blood of Jesus has washed my robes and made them white. He has purified me from all unrighteousness, and I am now a new creation in Him. I am empowered to overcome every obstacle and trial that may come my way, for I am a conqueror through Christ.

"From this day forward, I live in the fullness of Christ's victory. I am free from every oppression of satan. I am free from the captivity of fear, sin, and death. I am confident in Christ's love for me and His ability to lead me to triumph in every situation. With the assurance of salvation and the power of the Holy Spirit, I will live a life that brings glory to God's name, in Jesus' name."

12. Philippians 4:13 – "Christ is my source of strength, and example in all things. His Spirit empowers me to walk in victory every day. I refuse to be held down by any force of darkness. I arise with His help today and declare that I overcome any adversary and obstacle standing in my way. Henceforth, I can do all things through Him because He strengthens me daily.

13. Ephesians 1:7 – "Christ has set me free, saved me, made me unstoppable, and opened doors for me by His blood. He forgave my sins and broke the chains of darkness on the cross. I have the assurance of salvation and eternal life. I am empowered by the Holy Spirit to overcome any force of discouragement, rejection, and setback, in Jesus' name."

14. Hebrews 12:24 – "I declare my loyalty to Jesus, the divine mediator of a new covenant that unites God and humanity. I embrace the significance of His sprinkled blood, which echoes the message of forgiveness and speaks better things than the blood of Abel. I proclaim my liberation from every evil grip. I access the boundless grace and mercy of God.

"The blood of Jesus issues superior declarations over my life, which overshadows all evil accusations and condemnations that the enemy hurls at me, either now or in the future. I am a cherished child of God, a valued citizen of heaven, and a rightful heir to the promises of God."

15. 1 John 3:1 – "Through the blood of Jesus, I am a beloved child of God. I have received the spirit of adoption, by which I cry out, "Abba, Father." I am not of this world; I am of God; I belong to him. I am a partaker of His supernatural nature.

"I renounce every lie and deception attacking my mind and claim the truth that sets me free.

"I renounce all behaviors and addictions holding me captive and claim my victory through the power of the Holy Spirit.

"I am more than a conqueror.

"I have the mind of Christ, and I walk in his light.

"I have the power to resist every attack of the enemy.

"I walk in the freedom and victory God has given me."

16. Colossians 1:20 – "In Christ and His blood, I am reconciled to God. His sacrifice brought me forgiveness, redemption, and freedom. I am no longer under the dominion of darkness. I have been relocated to the kingdom where light prevails.

"From now onwards, I reject the enemy's lies and declare that Christ's deliverance extends to every area of my life. He has redeemed my mind from negative thoughts and renewed it with His truth. He has healed my brokenness and restored my heart. He has released me from all demonic chains and brought healing to my body.

"From today, I walk in the confidence of my deliverance, knowing that nothing can separate me from the love of God. I am more than a conqueror through Christ.

17. Hebrews 9:14 – "The blood of Jesus has cleansed my conscience from dead works and set me free from the bondage of wickedness. By faith, I have received the fullness of Christ's sacrifice. I am blessed and restored to a right relationship with God.

"The blood of Jesus not only cleanses me but also empowers me. Through the blood, I receive the life-giving Spirit of God, who enables me to live victoriously and walk in obedience to God's will.

"Today, I reject every accusation of the enemy and declare that I stand justified before God through the blood of Jesus. The blood of Jesus covers every area of my life, protects me from harm, delivers me from evil, and shields me from the attacks of the enemy, in Jesus' name."

18. Hebrews 10:22 – "In the name of Jesus, I release any feelings of guilt and shame, for the blood of Jesus has washed away my guiltiness and declared me righteous in God's sight. I am clothed in God's righteousness, and there is no condemnation against me that will stand.

"The blood of Jesus purifies my heart and conscience from all defilement. The blood has broken every evil restraint, shattered every captivity, and released me into a life of liberty and victory, in Jesus' name.

19. 1 Peter 1:2 – "I am the elect of God even before the foundation of the world. God chose me according to his foreknowledge and purpose. I am sanctified by the Holy Spirit, who sets me apart for God's service and transforms me into his image. I am made obedient to Christ, my Lord and Savior. I a member of the household of God, and a partaker of his inheritance, in Jesus' name.

20. Exodus 12:13 – "As I eat the flesh of Jesus and drink His blood, I apply the blood over the doorposts of my life, symbolically marking myself as one who belongs to Him, protected by His redeeming power.

"I declare that the blood is my shield and refuge, and no destructive plague can touch or overwhelm me.

"The blood of Jesus is a sign of my covenant relationship with God. I am covered and protected by His divine covenant of love, grace, and mercy. The blood of Jesus speaks a better word over my life, declaring me safe and secure in the shadow of my Heavenly Father, in Jesus' name.

MEDITATE ON THIS

*2. Colossians 2:14-15 –"**Christ has canceled all satanic charges against you by His blood. He has nullified all the legal indebtedness against you and your destiny.**"*

Chapter 5

The Blood of Jesus Speaks Against the Forces of Witchcraft

Luke 10:19 – *"God has given me the power and authority to overcome any obstacle or challenge that comes my way. No force of darkness or negativity can harm me or hinder my progress. I tread on the serpents and scorpions and overcome every power of the evil one. Nothing can stop me."*

I acknowledge that witchcraft is a harrowing spiritual battle, seeking to manipulate, control, and harm us through satanic powers and practices. But I also declare, with a steadfast heart, that as a believer, I have been given authority by God to overcome every power of the enemy. Through the blood of Jesus, I walk in victory and experience true freedom from every satanic manipulation.

Declarations

As I meditate and declare these Scriptures over my life, I experience victory over the forces of witchcraft. My trust lies in the power of the blood of Jesus, for it is through His blood that I conquer every attack and walk in the freedom and authority bestowed upon me in Christ.

1. **Isaiah 54:17** – "I declare that through the blood of Jesus, no weapon formed against me, not witchcraft, nor other devices of the enemy, shall prosper. Every spoken word made against me and my family is condemned,

rendered powerless, and destroyed forever and ever, in Jesus' name."

2. Psalm 59:8 – "My heavenly Father laughs at those who rise, sit, and gather together against me and the righteous cause. May His laughter drown every evil scheme against my life and destiny today and forever.

"I declare that by the blood of Jesus Christ, every satanic power attacking my life will be exposed and scorned, and their plans will be frustrated, in Jesus' name."

3. James 4:7 – "I am fully surrendered to God. By the power of the Holy Spirit, I resist the devil and the forces of witchcraft. May every stronghold of witchcraft and satanic manipulations against me and my home be destroyed. I command every enemy who has risen against me to lose their thoughts and abilities, in Jesus' name."

4. Numbers 23:23 – "I bring to nothing every enchantment and divination against my life and progress. By the blood of Jesus Christ, I cancel every evil declaration and curse pronounced against me by the forces of darkness. I declare them destroyed today and forever, in Jesus' name."

5. Psalm 27:1 – "Because the Lord is my light and my salvation, I nullify every satanic activity working to instill distress and confusion in my life and family. The Lord is the stronghold of my life, so the grip of fear, panic, worry, and satanic mutations are destroyed, in Jesus' name."

6. Luke 10:19 – "God has given me the power and authority to trample on serpents and scorpions, and over every strategy of the wicked one, and nothing shall by any means hurt me.

"I stand against every evil manipulation and witchcraft spell cast against me or anyone I know. I nullify them permanently.

"I command to be destroyed every demonic agenda over my life.

"I cancel every curse, hex, spell, incantation, and action initiated against me by witchcraft and satanic agents. They have no power over me. I overcome them all by the blood of Jesus Christ."

7. 2 Thessalonians 3:3 – "I declare that God is faithful. He has established me and commanded His protection over me and my household. No weapon formed against us shall prosper. We are blessed and highly favored.

8. Psalm 121:7 – "The Lord will keep me and my household from all evil; he will keep us safe by the blood of Jesus."

9. 1 John 4:4 – "I am of God, and have overcome satan, his agents, and the forces of witchcraft and their activities. For greater is Christ in me than them that are in the world.

10. 1 Corinthians 15:57 – "I give thanks to God; He gives me victory through my Lord Jesus Christ. I am not afraid of anything, including the human agents who parade themselves as witches, wizards, and occult men, because I know I am always victorious in Christ. I am strong and bold, and I will never give up. I will keep standing on my victory and never back down, for I am triumphant through Christ."

11. Psalm 118:14 – "The Lord is my strength and my song; He is my salvation and deliverance. To Him belongs all the glory, now and forever."

12. 1 Peter 2:9 – " I am a chosen child of God, a royal priest, a holy nation, and His own special people. I am called to proclaim His praises, for He has called me out of darkness into His marvelous light. By the blood of Jesus Christ, I am no longer a victim of the forces of witchcraft. I am empowered to live a life that honors God, and I will proclaim His praises throughout my life."

13. Deuteronomy 28:7 – "I am a child of the Most High God. I am blessed and highly favored. I am the head and not the tail. I am above and not beneath. I am a new creation in Christ Jesus. Everything old has passed away, and everything new has come. I have received the blessings of Abraham, and I am now living a brand new life.

"When I come in, I am blessed, and when I go out, I am blessed. When enemies rise against me, the Lord makes sure they lose. Each time they come against me in one way, God will cause them to flee before me in seven ways.

"The Lord has commanded His blessing upon my storehouses, and everything I set my hand to do prospers. I will walk in divine health, supernatural provision, and protection."

14. Isaiah 41:10 – "God is my strength and my shield. He will strengthen me and help me. He will sustain me with His righteous right hand. Therefore, I will not be afraid, for He is with me. He is my God and my protector. No work of satan will thrive against me. I am born of God. The blood of Jesus protects and covers me every day.

15. 2 Corinthians 10:3-4 – "I recognize and confess that the battles I face are not against physical humans. Thankfully, the weapons at my disposal transcend man-made tools and strategies. My weapons are powerful to pull down even the strongest stronghold. Today, I apply the weapon of the blood of Jesus Christ and declare every demonic stronghold that has empowered the activities of witchcraft in my life and in my home destroyed, in Jesus' name.

16. John 10:10 – "Lord Jesus, you are the Good Shepherd who came that I may have life and have it abundantly. Today, I take back everything the thief has stolen from me through any form of witchcraft activity and demonic manipulation. I declare that I walk in your abundant provision, healing, and restoration.

"I walk in victory every day through the speaking blood of Jesus Christ and the power of the Holy Spirit.

"I am blessed when I go out and come in. Every need of mine is supernaturally met according to the riches in glory by Christ Jesus.

"I am restored in every area of my life. My health is restored, my mind is restored, my relationships are restored, and my finances are restored, in Jesus' name."

17. Romans 8:37 – "By the blood of Jesus Christ, the love and mercy of God, I am more than a conqueror. I live in faith above the works of satan and witchcraft, in Jesus' name."

18. Deuteronomy 18:10 – "Father, Your Word says there shall not be found among us anyone who causes his son or his daughter to pass through the fire, one who practices witchcraft, or a soothsayer, or one who reads omens, or an enchanter, or one who invokes spirits, casts a spell, or calls up the dead.

"I declare that I have nothing to do with witchcraft or the occult. I renounce all involvement in these practices, whether past or present. I repent of any past curiosity or experimentation with these things.

"By the blood of Jesus, I renounce curses, spells, hexes, charms, and wishcrafts sent against me through witchcraft practices. I declare that the blood of Jesus sets me free from every bondage and protects me. I belong to Christ, seated with Him in the heavenly places, far above all principalities and powers, authorities and dominions. I am untouchable, in Jesus' name.

Father, let Your holy fire consume every work of darkness against my family and me, and let Your angels encamp around us, protecting us from all harm, in Jesus' name."

19. Galatians 5:19-21 – "By the blood of Jesus Christ, I claim my victory over the works of the flesh, which are sexual immorality, impure thoughts, indecency, idolatry, sorcery, resentment, quarreling, jealousy, outbursts of anger, selfishness, dissension, division, envy, witchcraft, drunkenness, wild parties, and other sins like these. I declare total victory and say: I want nothing to do with these works of darkness.

"I claim the fruit of the Spirit: love, joy, peace, patience, kindness, goodness, faithfulness, gentleness, and self-control. I declare that these qualities abound in me today and every day, in Jesus' name."

20. Acts 19:18-19 – "In the mighty name of Jesus, I expose and relinquish every association with the powers of darkness seeking to manipulate and control my life. By the authority of the blood of Jesus, I am freed from the clutches of witchcraft and its deceitful entanglements.

"May any materials, rings, ornaments, clothes, symbols, marks, books, tools, and instruments associated with witchcraft, idolatry, and magic, currently in my possession, knowingly or unknowingly, be exposed and consumed by fire from heaven.

"I proclaim my separation from these works of darkness; I sever all ties and bonds they once held over me. Through the power of the blood of Jesus, I nullify their influence and render them worthless.

"As divine flames devour the remnants of my past entanglements, I arise as a victorious warrior, liberated from the chains of darkness. I embrace the fullness of Christ's deliverance, walking in the light of His truth. I am no longer bound by the powers of darkness, for the blood of Jesus has set me free.

"I decree and declare that every curse, every covenant, and every soul tie associated with witchcraft is now permanently broken. I am cleansed, purified, and sanctified by the precious blood of Jesus Christ. My path is cleared, and my destiny is secured in the hands of my Savior, Jesus Christ.

"Henceforth, by this Communion, I am clothed in the armor of God and empowered by the Holy Spirit. My life is a living testimony of the transforming grace of God. I am an instrument of His righteousness, spreading the fragrance of freedom and victory wherever I go, in Jesus' name.

MEDITATE ON THIS

*Psalm 121:7 – **"The Lord will keep you and your family from all evil; he will keep you safe by the blood of Jesus."***

Chapter 6

Total Deliverance By the Blood

Colossians 1:13 – *"I am no longer under the control of the devil. I have been delivered from his domain and translated into the kingdom of God's beloved Son. I am free from the lies and deception of the enemy. His schemes and temptations no longer bind me. I am free to live in the light of God's truth."*

I am called out of darkness into Christ's marvelous light. I have the authority to trample on snakes and scorpions and overcome all the power of the enemy. I am spiritually armed and equipped with formidable weapons that trash every scheme of the devil. I have the sword of the Spirit, which is the word of God, to speak against every lie and accusation of the enemy.

Today, as I take the Holy Communion, I remind myself that I am connected to Christ. What I eat is not a mere ritual or mere bread and wine. It is the flesh and blood of Jesus. I use it to remind myself that Jesus Christ died for me on the cross, resurrected on the third day, and will come again to establish his kingdom forever and ever.

By this communion, I declare my submission to God and the authority of His Word. As I declare the following scriptures over my life and situations, I end every work of darkness and release God's transformative power over everything that concerns me, in Jesus' name.

1. Speak Against Soul Ties

1 Corinthians 6:16-17 - "In the name of Jesus Christ, I declare that I am united with the Lord in spirit. I call forth the blood of Jesus to speak against every satanic soul tie in my life. I renounce and break every evil soul tie, knowingly or unknowingly, formed between me and any person, place, thing, or spirit that is not of God.

"I sever every connection and influence contrary to God's will and purpose for my life.

"I receive the cleansing and healing of the blood of Jesus Christ over my soul, mind, will, and emotions. I am free from every soulish bondage and entanglement, in Jesus' name."

2. Speak Against Marine Witchcraft

Psalm 89:9 – "In the name of Jesus Christ, I call forth the blood of Jesus to speak against marine spirits and witchcraft against my life and family. I declare that I am delivered from every water spirit assigned to attack, oppress, and deceive me. I rebuke and bind the demonic forces of leviathans, pythons, mermaid spirits, and any other aquatic demons strategizing and fighting against the plan and purpose of God for my life, family, and environment. in my life and environment. I command them to be silenced and cast into the abyss, in Jesus' name.

"I release the fire of God to consume every altar, covenant, and agreement made with these spirits. I declare that I am under the authority and protection of Jesus Christ, who rules over the surging seas, in Jesus' name."

3. Speak Against Generational Curses

Galatians 3:13 – "Blood of Jesus, speak against any types of generational curses speaking against my life and family.

"I plead the blood of Jesus over my life and family lineage. I declare that I am delivered from every generational curse passed down to me by my ancestors.

"By the blood of Jesus, I cancel every legal right and access the enemy has gained through sin, disobedience, idolatry, murder, suicide, and ignorance.

"I break every cycle and pattern of failure, poverty, sickness, addiction, divorce, and other curses in my family. I declare that I and my family are blessed with every spiritual blessing in Christ Jesus. The curses of the law are broken, and we are enrolled as partakers of the blessings of Abraham, in Jesus' name."

4. Speak Against Familiar Spirits

Leviticus 19:31 – "Blood of Jesus Christ, speak against every familiar spirit sent to spy on me, manipulate me, or harm me. I renounce and reject any contact or communication that I have had with any medium, spiritist, psychic, witch doctor, fortune teller, or any other agent of darkness.

"I repent of any involvement or interest I had shown in occultism, divination, sorcery, magic, or witchcraft.

"I command every familiar spirit to leave me alone and never return in Jesus' name.

"I declare that I am sanctified by the blood of Jesus Christ. I am led daily by the Holy Spirit, and He reveals to me all things that pertain to life and godliness.

5. Speak Against Monitoring Spirits

1 Peter 3:12 – "Blood of Jesus Christ, speak against every monitoring spirit assigned to watch, track, or report on my movements, activities, or progress. Expose and destroy every device, gadget, or instrument planted or used by these spirits to monitor me.

"In the name of Jesus, I blind and deafen every evil eye and ear spying and eavesdropping on me. I declare that no weapon designed against me and my household shall prosper, and every evil word against us is now condemned.

"The eyes of the Lord are on me, and his ears are attentive to my prayers. His face is against those who concoct evil against me and my family, in Jesus' name."

6. Speak Against Evil Dreams

Psalm 4:8 – "Blood of Jesus, speak against evil dreams sent to torment, frighten, and confuse me. Nullify every adverse effect and consequence of demonic dreams that I've had in the past.

"I command the evil spirits released through the bad dreams in my life to leave me now and never return.

"I declare that I have the mind of Christ and the peace of God that surpasses all understanding.

"From today, I will lie down and sleep in peace, for the Lord alone makes me dwell in safety and gives me good sleep. My dreams shall be revelations from God, in Jesus' name."

7. Speak Against Dream Stealers

John 10:10 – "Though satan, the thief, has come to steal, kill, and destroy, my Lord and Savior, Jesus Christ, has come to give me life and a life that lacks nothing, but has all good things in abundance."

"Blood of Jesus, speak against dream stealers and star manipulators sent to rob me of my destiny, purpose, and inheritance. I recover and restore everything stolen from me through manipulation in times past.

"I command every spirit of delay, denial, diversion, and destruction to be bound and cast out of my life and into the abyss, in Jesus' name.

"I declare that I have life and have it to the full. I have the power and ability to fulfill my God-given dreams."

8. Speak Against Demonic Obstacles

Romans 8:31 – "Blood of Jesus, speak against demonic obstacles placed on my way to hinder, block, and stop me from advancing in God's will for my life. Remove and demolish demonic barriers, walls, mountains, and evil gates erected by the enemy to oppose me in my finances, ministry, and home.

"I declare that God is for me and with me. Therefore, no one and nothing can stand against me.

9. Speak Against Witchcraft Attacks

1 John 4:4 – "The One who dwells within me, the Almighty God, is infinitely greater than any witchcraft in this world. I embrace my identity as a beloved child of God. I refuse to be defined by the threats and attacks from the enemy, for the power of God flows through my very being. The forces seeking to stop me are no match for the indomitable presence of the Almighty in me and with me."

"I, therefore, call forth the Blood of Jesus to speak against every witchcraft attack launched against me by any person, group, or organization.

"I command fire to destroy every spell, enchantment, bewitchment, and manipulation sent to harm or control me.

"I command every witchcraft spirit released against my life and into my family to loose their hold and be cast into the fire, in Jesus' name."

10. Speak Against Ancestral Spirits

Hebrews 6:1-2 – "It's time for me to progress beyond the basic teachings of Christ and continue to grow in maturity. I refuse to settle on the foundational principle of repentance from dead works, demons, and deliverance, for I have already experienced the transformative power of God's redemption.

"I choose to advance in my spiritual journey. I embrace the call to deeper understanding and maturity. I will not be held back by the past or linger in surface knowledge. I receive grace and empowerment of the Holy Spirit to explore the profound truths and experience the fullness of God's love and grace."

"Today, I call forth the Blood of Jesus to speak against ancestral spirits claiming ownership or authority over my life and lineage. I renounce and reject any allegiance or affiliation with any idol, shrine, altar, or covenant made by my ancestors with these spirits.

"I declare that I belong to God and God alone. He is my Father and my God. He is the God of the living and not the dead. So, I command every ancestral spirit to release me and let me go. I want to focus on deeper scriptural realities from now onwards, in Jesus' name."

11. Speak Against Spirit Spouse

Isaiah 54:5 – "I declare that I am God's own. Therefore, I call forth the Blood of Jesus to speak against every spirit husband or wife claiming marital rights or intimacy with me.

"I renounce and divorce every spirit spouse assigned to me by the enemy. I break every covenant, contract, and agreement made with these spirits, knowingly or unknowingly.

"I command every spirit husband or wife to pack their load and leave my life and family alone, in Jesus' name.

"I am married to the Lord Almighty, my Maker and Redeemer. He is the God of heaven and earth, and no one can contend with him."

12. Speak Against False Prophets

2 Peter 2:1 –" Blood of Jesus, speak against false prophets and teachers sent to deceive, mislead, and exploit me or any member of my family. Cause us to discern and reject every doctrine of demons, every lie of the enemy, and every counterfeit of the truth.

"I command every spirit of error, deception, confusion, and manipulation attacking my mind and the minds of my family members to be exposed and cast out, in Jesus' name.

"I declare that we have the Spirit of truth, who guides us into all truth. We have the mind of Christ, who teaches us all things, in Jesus' name."

13. Speak Against Fear and Torment

2 Timothy 1:7 – "Blood of Jesus, speak against every spirit of fear and torment sent to paralyze, intimidate, harass, and cause me to withdraw from projects and activities designed to bless and lift me.

"I rebuke and cast out the evil spirits of fear, anxiety, worry, panic, dread, phobia, and terror from me and my family and send them to the abyss. I declare that we did not receive a spirit of fear but of love, power, and a sound mind, in Jesus' name."

14. Speak Against Sickness and Disease

1 **Peter 2:24** – "Blood of Jesus, speak against sicknesses and diseases sent to afflict, weaken, and destroy me. Uproot the spirits of infirmity, pain, and suffering from me and my family.

"I command every sickness and disease attacking me and my household to dry up and die at the root, in Jesus' name.

"I declare that we are healed by the stripes of Jesus Christ. No disease shall come near our abode anymore, in Jesus' name.

15. Speak Against Lack and Poverty

2 Corinthians 8:9 – "Blood of Jesus, speak against the spirit of poverty that robs us of abundance, prosperity, and blessing.

"In Jesus name, I rebuke and cast out the spirits of lack, debt, and insufficiency from my life and family. I break every curse of poverty speaking against me and my household.

"I declare that God makes all grace abound to me; I will have all sufficiency in all good things at all times. I will abound in every good work and will not be stopped by lack, in Jesus' name."

16. SpeakAgainst Oppression

Isaiah 61:1 – "Blood of Jesus Christ, speak against the spirit of oppression that crushes, burdens, and enslaves.

"I command and cast out the spirits of heaviness, depression, and despair from my life and family. May every evil yoke and bondage in my life and family be broken and destroyed, in Jesus' name.

"I declare that the Spirit of the Lord God is upon me; He has anointed me to bring good news to the poor. He has sent me to bind up the heartbroken, to announce freedom to the captives, and the opening of the prison to those who are bound. Thank You, Jesus."

17. Speak Against Rejection

1 Peter 2:9 – "Blood of Jesus, speak against the spirit of rejection that wounds, isolates, and discourages. Speak healing over every damage caused by rejection in me and my family. From today, I command the spirit of rejection to leave me and my family now and never return, in Jesus' name.

"I declare that we are a chosen people, a royal priesthood, a holy nation, a people for the Lord's possession. God loves us and has drawn us with unfailing kindness."

18. Speak Against Anger

Ephesians 4:26 – "By the blood of Jesus Christ, I am free from the spirit of anger that provokes, inflames, and consumes. I renounce and repent of any sin I have committed in anger, and I command the spirit of anger to leave me now and never return, in Jesus' name.

19. Speak Against Bitterness

Ephesians 4:31-32 – "By the blood of Jesus Christ, I declare that I am free from the spirit of bitterness and unforgiveness sent to poison, defile, and torment me.

"I speak healing over any wound that bitterness and unforgiveness have inflicted on me, either by others or by myself. I command the foul spirits of bitterness and unforgiveness to leave me now and never return.

"I declare that I have the grace and mercy of God to forgive others as he has forgiven me."

20. Speak Against Pride and Arrogance

Proverbs 16:18 says that "Pride goes before destruction, a haughty spirit before a fall."

"Today, I call forth the Blood of Jesus to speak against the spirit of pride and arrogance that deceives, puffs up, and destroys. May the

Blood wash my heart and mind and empower me to always humble myself and trust in God's ways, not my own ways.

"I embrace the example set by Jesus Christ, who, in his immeasurable love and humility, willingly humbled himself to death on the cross. I willingly surrender my desires and aspirations at his feet and reject every allure of selfish ambition and the pursuit of personal gain.

"I declare that I am empowered by the same Spirit in Christ. I choose to walk in his footsteps, embracing his humility and grace. I will not cling to worldly status or seek recognition for my own glory. May my daily decisions and actions reflect his humility and selflessness.

"I declare that I am empowered by the Holy Spirit to lay aside pride, arrogance, and the paraphernalia of this world. In the face of challenges and temptations, I stand firm in the assurance that I can draw from the Spirit of Christ's love and humility. I resist the forces that seek to exalt self and remind myself to always walk in humility, love, and compassion.

"I declare that I have the fear of the Lord, which is the beginning of wisdom. I have the humility of Christ, which commands divine promotion. I will be a blessing to others. My gifts and abilities bless my community and generation, in Jesus' name."

Thank You, Jesus, for delivering me from every work of darkness by Your blood. Be praised forever and ever, in Jesus name.

Amen.

MEDITATE ON THIS

*Philippians 2:8 – **"And being found in appearance as a man, he humbled himself by becoming obedient to death - even death on a cross!"***

Chapter 7

All-Around Blessings By the Blood of Jesus

Hebrews 13:20-21 – *"The God of peace, who raised our Lord Jesus from the dead, has equipped me with everything good to do His will. He is working in me, making me pleasing in His sight through Jesus Christ, to whom be all glory forever and ever. Amen."*

I am blessed with every spiritual blessing in the heavenly places. My sins are forgiven. I am a child of God. I have peace with God and access to His grace and mercy.

By the Holy Communion – the flesh and the blood of Jesus Christ – my physical and material needs are supernaturally met. I access grace and power for living a wealthy and blessed life.

God supplies all my needs according to His riches in glory by Christ Jesus. He is granting me the desires of my heart. I will prosper in all that I do, and I will be successful in everything I set my mind to.

By the blood of Jesus Christ, I am empowered to command blessings over my life and family, and it will be so. I can declare that I am healthy, wealthy, and wise. I can declare that I have peace, joy, and love. I can declare that I am successful in my career and my relationships.

Whatever I decree and declare stands so in heaven and earth.

Today, I take the Holy Communion and stand on God's word to declare His blessings over my life, family, and everything that concerns me. I declare these scriptures and stand on their power and reality. It will happen to me just as I decree.

Declarations

1. Psalm 5:12 – "By the blood of Jesus, I declare that I am the righteousness of God in Christ. Therefore, I am blessed and divinely favored.

"Every closed door is now open. I see blessings overflow into my life. I see supernatural connections, opportunities, and breakthroughs in every area of my life, in Jesus' name."

2. 3 John 1:2 – "Through the blood of Jesus, I am free from sicknesses and diseases. I receive the divine health that Christ purchased for me on the cross. Every cell, organ, and system in my body perfectly aligns with God's original design. I walk in divine health. Every aspect of my life prospers even as my soul prospers, in Jesus' name."

3. Isaiah 40:31 – "By the blood of Jesus Christ, my strength is supernaturally renewed every morning. I mount up with wings like eagles. I soar above every limitation and obstacle. I run with divine speed. Weariness has no place in my life. I walk in the supernatural strength of the Lord, accomplishing great things for His glory, in Jesus' name."

4. Isaiah 43:19 – "Through the blood of Jesus, I declare that God is doing a new thing in my life. He is making a way where there is no way. I fix my eyes on His promises and trust in His faithfulness. I will walk in His supernatural breakthrough as He opens doors, even in places that hitherto looked like wilderness. My desert places will bring forth refreshing streams, even as the blood of Jesus paves the way for miraculous transformation in every area of my life, in Jesus' name."

5. Joel 2:25 – "By the blood of Jesus Christ, I declare restoration in my life; I declare restoration for the years that the devourers have stolen. I proclaim divine redemption over every loss, setback, and disappointment I have suffered.

"I declare double restoration for the years the enemy has tried to destroy. I declare that my life is a testimony of divine turnaround, for everything is now turning around for my good. Henceforth, I am positioned for unprecedented interventions and open doors, in Jesus' name."

6. Malachi 3:10 – "Through the blood of Jesus Christ, I declare that I am a faithful steward of what God has entrusted me. I honor God with my tithes and offerings. Therefore, I receive the fullness of God's blessing over my finances. I walk in financial abundance. The windows of heaven are open for me. I receive an outpouring of ideas, favors, divine help, and opportunities, in Jesus' name."

7. Psalm 133:1 – "By the blood of Jesus, I declare that I am an agent of reconciliation. I walk in harmony with my brothers and sisters in Christ. I walk in forgiveness and extend love and grace to others.

"As I seek peace, unity, and reconciliation, God blesses me. Divine connections, divine relationships, and divine alignments are established in my life, bringing forth supernatural increase, and abundance, in Jesus' name."

8. Psalm 46:1 – "God is my refuge and strength. He is an ever-present help in trouble. In the face of challenges, I will not be shaken, for He is with me. His power and presence go before me every day and make crooked places straight. I will walk in victory in every situation, in Jesus' name."

9. Deuteronomy 8:18 – "By the power of the blood of Jesus, I declare that I am a covenant child of God. I receive from God and possess the ability to create wealth and influence through His help. I enjoy supernatural supplies, breakthroughs, and abundance.

"From now onwards, every venture and endeavor I undertake will prosper beyond human understanding because God has empowered me to create wealth to fulfill His purpose on the earth."

10. Philippians 4:19 – "God supplies all my need according to His riches in glory by Christ. I lack nothing, for God is my provider. Every area of my life is abundantly provided for. I am a channel of blessings, and God's abundant provision flows through me to impact others, in Jesus' name."

11. Proverbs 16:7 – "By the blood of Jesus, I declare that I am a peacemaker. God takes pleasure in my ways and causes my enemies to make peace with me. Every form of opposition, strife, and conflict in my life and family is silenced forever. I receive grace to walk in supernatural harmony in my relationships, in Jesus' name."

12. Psalm 1:3 – "Through the blood of Jesus, I declare that I am firmly rooted in Christ, like a tree planted by streams of living water. I bear fruit in due season, and everything I put my hands to do prospers. My life is fruitful and impactful; I am sustained by the Word of God and the power of the Holy Spirit. I bring forth a harvest of righteousness and blessings in every area of my life, in Jesus' name."

13. Proverbs 18:22 – "I declare that I am divinely connected to my spouse. We have a godly relationship characterized by love, understanding, and unity. The favor of the Lord rests upon my marriage, and our relationship reflects the beauty of Christ's love for His church. Our union is a testimony of the redemptive power of the blood of Jesus, in Jesus' name."

14. Psalm 23:6 – "Through the blood of Jesus, goodness and mercy shall follow me all the days of my life. God's favor surrounds me like a shield. I will dwell in the house of the

Lord; I abide in His presence, experience His divine nature, and flourish in His courts. My life will overflow with the goodness of God every day, in Jesus' name."

15. Jeremiah 33:3 – "By the power of the blood of Jesus, I declare that I have access to the throne of God. God answers my prayers and declarations and reveals hidden mysteries and divine secrets to me. I walk in supernatural wisdom, revelation, knowledge, and strategies. From today, I access divine insights that produce uncommon breakthroughs and success. My life is marked by divine intelligence, in Jesus' name."

16. Psalm 92:12-14 – "Through the blood of Jesus, I declare that I am righteous and planted in the house of the Lord. I flourish like a palm tree and grow like a cedar of Lebanon. I am fruitful and impactful, no matter my age or circumstances. My life remains fresh and green, filled with divine vitality and strength. I leave a lasting legacy that glorifies God and blesses generations to come, in Jesus' name."

17. Proverbs 3:5-6 – "I declare that I trust in the Lord with all my heart. I do not rely on my own understanding; I submit every aspect of my life to Him. As I surrender to His will, He directs my paths and makes them straight. I will walk in His guidance and discernment, and every step I take will be ordered by Him, in Jesus' name."

18. Proverbs 10:22 – "I declare that the blessing of the Lord makes me rich, and adds no sorrow to me. I walk in prosperity; God's blessing rests upon every area of my life and family. I experience the joy and fulfillment of walking in alignment with God's principles of abundance. The blood of Jesus shields me from any form of sorrow and lack, in Jesus' name."

19. Philippians 4:13 – "I can do all things through Christ who strengthens me. I am empowered by the indwelling Spirit of God to overcome every obstacle and accomplish every task set before me. I walk in supernatural strength and resilience, and triumph in every situation, in Jesus' name."

20. Ephesians 3:20 – "Through the blood of Jesus, I declare that God will do immeasurably more than all I ask or imagine, according to His power at work within me. I am a vessel of God's unlimited power and potential. I dare to dream big, knowing that God's plans for my life surpass my wildest imagination. I walk in divine manifestations of breakthroughs that bring glory to His name. The blood of Jesus activates God's supernatural abundance in my life, in Jesus' name."

Amen.

MEDITATE ON THIS

*Isaiah 40:31 – **"But they that wait upon the Lord shall renew their strength; they shall mount up with wings as eagles; they shall run, and not be weary; and they shall walk, and not faint."***

BOOKS BY THE SAME AUTHOR

Prayers to Cancel Disappointments at the Edge of Breakthrough

Prayers to Cancel the Curse of Marital Delay

Prayers to Remove Yourself from Negative Generational Patterns

31 Days in the School of Faith

31 Days With the Heroes of Faith

31 Days With the Holy Spirit

31 Days With Jesus

31 Days in the Parables

None of These Diseases

I Will Arise and Shine

Psalm 91

Prayer Retreat:
HEALING PRAYERS & CONFESSIONS
200 Violent Prayers
Hearing God's Voice in Painful Moments
Healing Prayers
Healing WORDS

Prayers That Break Curses

120 Powerful Night Prayers

How to Pray for Your Children Everyday

How to Pray for Your Family

Daily Prayer Guide

Make Him Respect You

How to Cast Out Demons from Your Home, Office & Property

Praying Through the Book of Psalms

The Students' Prayer Book

How to Pray and Receive Financial Miracle

Powerful Prayers to Destroy Witchcraft Attacks.

Deliverance from Marine Spirits

Deliverance From Python Spirit

Anger Management God's Way

How God Speaks to You

Deliverance of the Mind

20 Commonly Asked Questions About Demons

Praying the Promises of God

When God Is Silent

I SHALL NOT DIE

Praise Warfare

Prayers to Find a Godly Spouse

How to Exercise Authority Over Sickness

Under His Shadow

GET IN TOUCH

We love testimonies. So, please share how this book or other of my books has inspired or helped you. Connect with me on social media:

Facebook: www.facebook.com/drdanielokpara

Instagram: @drdanielokpara

Telegram: https://t.me/mybetterlifetoday

Also, please consider checking out my other books on Amazon:

amazon.com/author/danielokpara .

Visit our website, www.BetterLifeWorld.org, and send us your prayer request. As we join faith with you, God's power will be made manifest in your life.

ABOUT THE AUTHOR

Daniel Chika Okpara's life assignment is to make lives better by teaching and preaching God's Word with signs and wonders. He is the resident pastor of Shining Light Christian Centre, a fast-growing church in Lagos. He is also the president and CEO of Better Life World Outreach Center, a non-denominational ministry dedicated to evangelism, prayer, and empowering God's people with the WORD and tools to make their lives better.

Daniel Okpara has authored over 100 life-transforming books and manuals on business, prayer, relationships, and victorious living, many of which have become best-sellers on Amazon and other bookstores.

He is a Computer Engineer by training and holds a master's degree in Christian Education from Continental Christian University. He is married, and they are blessed with lovely children.

WEBSITE: www.betterlifeworld.org

FREE BOOKS

To appreciate you obtaining this book, I'm offering you these four powerful books today for free. Download them on our website and take your relationship with God to a new level.

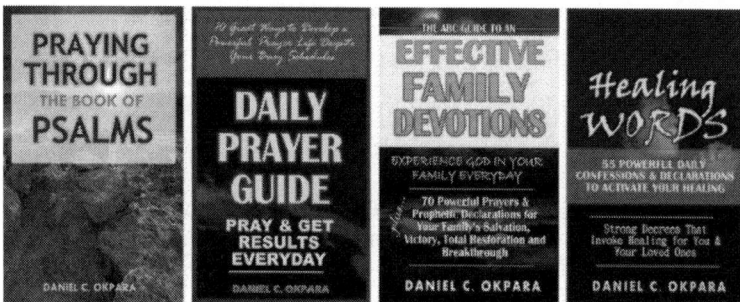

Click Here to Download

www.betterlifeworld.org/grow

NOTES

1b642351-254f-4900-b534-a52d86e2a1a1R01